MW00512758

Beginners Stock Market Investing

How Beginners and Advanced Traders Can Succeed In Stocks

MORRIS DEVEY

Table of Contents

Introduction

This book is an excellent beginner's guide to understand the fundamentals of the stock market. First, we'll analyze the top five large tech stocks; Microsoft, Amazon, Apple, Facebook, and Alphabet or Google and also perform a stock valuation on each of them, so you can get a sense of what their current fair value ranges might be. To do that, we'll use my custom value stock valuation model to help us in that valuation process. Next, we will look at five specific stocks and discuss several investment considerations, including both the risks and opportunities for each stock over the next five years. After that, I'll be sharing five of my favorite stocks - all of which I have owned that can help generate long-term returns for your portfolio year after year. Next, we will take a look at three stocks under $5 per share for long term investing, five stocks to buy for higher upside, seven Dividend Stocks to Pay Your Rent, the five best Health Care Stocks, five NFT Stocks and the top seven Cash Flow Dividend Stocks. Next you will learn how to deal with

Stock Volatility, how to deal with a falling Stock and how to use Tax-Efficient Fund Placement which is one of the few ways that you can increase the return from your portfolio without impacting the risk, and you can do this by minimizing the total tax burden of your portfolio over time. We we'll cover an overview of tax efficient fund placement, what it is, the general strategy, and how you can put it into practice to start saving you money. You will also learn about the top five IT Index Funds, the best four Emerging Market ETFs, five Clean Energy ETFs, the best five Crypto Mining Stocks and the five most performing REIT Index Funds & ETFs. Finally, we will cover my top seven Penny Stocks for Commodities super cycle.

Chapter 1
Top 5 Tech Stocks

In this chapter we'll take a look at and analyze the top five large tech stocks Microsoft, Amazon, Apple, Facebook, and Alphabet or Google and also perform a stock valuation on each of them so you can get a sense of what their current fair value ranges might be. To do that, we'll use my custom value stock valuation model to help us in that valuation process. The value seeker model is a discounted earnings Model, so it effectively projects the future earnings for a company and then calculates what's the fair value price you need to pay today in order to achieve a specified rate of return. In the case of Facebook, we're just looking at a base case scenario and, in this case, we'll be looking at a modeling period over five years and we'll make some assumptions on Facebook's earnings growth over the next five years. In this case we assume earnings will increase 10% the next year, then starting in year two they'll increase 13% for each of the next four years. The model then uses that information to calculate an annualized earnings growth rate, we input our current earnings per share figure that earnings per share growth has been projected out over the next five years.

B	C	D	E	F		H	I	J
Model Duration (Years):		5						
(Stage 1) Modeled Earnings Growth Rate:		10.0%				Fair Valuation (at 12% RRR):		$216.71
(Stage 2) Modeled Earnings Growth Rate:		13.0%				Current Price:		$251.96
Stage 2 Earnings Growth Rate Start Year:		2				Margin of Safety (%):		0%
						Overvalued (%):		16%
5 Year Annualized Earnings Growth Rate:	0.0%	12.7%	0.0%			Upside to Fair Value (%):		0%
5-Year Total Earnings Growth:	0.0%	230.4%	0.0%			Downside Risk (%):		-14%
Current Annual EPS:	$8.19	$8.19	$8.19			Year	EPS	Dividends
Modeled Share Reduction % Per Year:		0.0%				Start	$8.19	$0.00
(Stage 1) Calculated EPS Growth Rate:	0.0%	10.0%	0.0%			1	$9.01	$0.00
(Stage 2) Calculated EPS Growth Rate:	0.0%	13.0%	0.0%			2	$10.18	$0.00
Average 5-Year EPS Growth Rate:	0.0%	12.7%	0.0%			3	$11.50	$0.00
						4	$13.00	$0.00
Current Annual Dividend:	$0.00	$0.00	$0.00			5	$14.69	$0.00
Current Annual Dividend Yield:	0.0%	0.0%	0.0%					

In this case Facebook does not pay a dividend so we're setting this just at zero. For this model we're targeting a 12% rate of return, and this can be different based on your return expectations or what rate of return you're targeting. Keep in mind that having a higher required rate of return means you'll need to buy at a lower price and vice versa. Finally, the last input is the expected price to earnings ratio at the end of the modeling period in this case we're modelling Facebook will end at a 26 price to earnings ratio. The model's calculated fair value is roughly $217. The way this is calculated is that assuming all the model assumptions are true, this is the price you'd need to pay today in order to achieve that 12% annualized rate of return over the entire five years. This would result in an expected price of Facebook in five years of roughly $382 dollars with no reinvested dividends since Facebook does not currently pay a dividend. The model can then compare this to the current price of the stock to determine if the stock is trading above that fair valuation or trading below potentially giving you a margin of safety with your investment. This graph is helpful for understanding how much of the return component is coming from different factors, namely earnings growth, valuation change, and dividends reinvested over time.

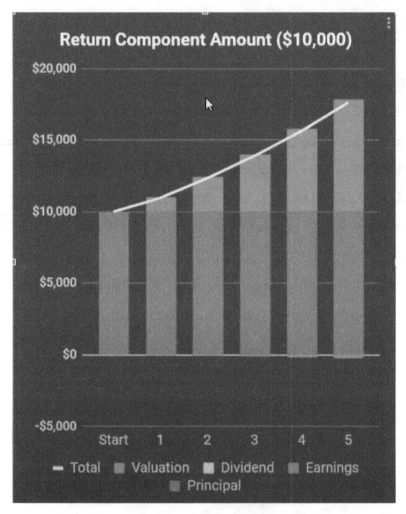

Starting with Facebook - as you know owns the world's largest social media platforms. The most profitable of which is Facebook which has almost 1.8 billion users every day. Across their family of products which includes Facebook, Instagram, Messenger, and WhatsApp, in the second quarter of

2020, almost two and a half billion people used at least one of their products every day.

Family Daily Active People (DAP)
In Billions

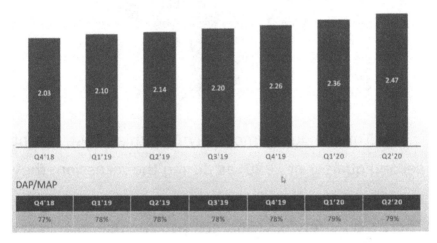

Facebook makes the majority of their money running ads for their users so the formula for total revenue of Facebook is pretty straightforward - it's just the average revenue per person, times the number of people that are using the site. Generally, as Facebook's been able to increase both the number of active users and the average revenue per user, they've been able to see strong revenue growth over the years.

Revenue

In Millions

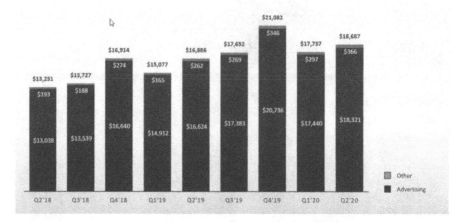

This is quite impressive in this most recent second quarter of 2020, as during the recession, they were actually able to increase revenues by 11%. There's a variety of resources you can use to help set your assumptions for earnings growth over time. Generally speaking, the more conservative you are in assumption setting, a lower fair value estimate will be produced. Over the past five years Facebook has been able to grow earnings well in excess of 13% per year, but in this case, I've set a relatively conservative assumption assuming they hit 13% growth rate from years 2 through 5. For the first year I took off just a bit of that growth rate, assuming that rates are likely slower during the recession although they have been quite robust so far. The 12% required wave return again is what we're using for this analysis, and a terminal price earnings ratio at 26, which is lower than what it's trading at now, but I do expect that growth will likely slow down at some point in the future so a lower price to earnings multiple should reflect that. Overall, with this relatively conservative modelling, a price of $217 for Facebook seems to be an attractive value for long-term investors. If you have different assumptions on the long-term growth rate for Facebook, let's say assuming 15% instead of 13%, well then, that fair valuation changes to 232 dollars. And if you're willing to pay a higher price and accept a lower expected rate of return, for instance in this case let's say 10% per year, then you have a fair valuation price at that 10% rate of return of 254 dollars per share which in this case is above the current price, meaning it would make sense assuming these assumptions hold true to buy the stock. There's often a lot of discussion that the fang stocks and many growth stocks are quite expensive, but I think it helps actually doing some real model and valuation work and calculate what actually would be a reasonable price based on your assumptions.

The next stock I want to look at is Alphabet, whose main property is Google. In the second quarter of June 2020 for the first time in its history as a public company Alphabet or Google, reported a decrease in revenue.

	Quarter Ended June 30,	
	2019	2020
Revenues	$38,944	$38,297
Increase (decrease) in revenues year over year	19 %	(2)%
Increase (decrease) in constant currency revenues year over year[1]	22 %	0 %
Operating income	$9,180	$6,383
Operating margin	24 %	17 %
Other income (expense), net	$2,967	$1,894
Net income	$9,947	$6,959
Diluted EPS	$14.21	$10.13

[1] Non-GAAP measure. See the table captioned "Reconciliation from GAAP revenues to non-GAAP constant currency revenues" for more details.

In this case revenue for the quarter was down roughly 2%, compared to the quarter a year ago. Part of the reason why Facebook has been more resilient in the recession compared to Google when both are in the online advertising space, is that when it comes to the specific ads being run on these sites, Facebook is a lot more focused on direct response advertising. This is designed to get consumers to either click a link or buy a product or download an app or something along the lines of an immediate action. Brand advertising on the other hand is more of a long-term investment. As brand advertising is estimated to make up roughly 80% of YouTube ad spend, it makes sense that Google might be more impacted here, as advertising budgets are shrunk and more focused on the immediate return of direct response advertising. In addition to this, the largest money maker for Alphabet is Google's search and some of the highest paying search terms are for travel and autos, which have seen significant declines during this recession.

	Quarter Ended June 30,	
	2019	2020
Google Search & other	$23,642	$21,319
YouTube ads[1]	3,603	3,812
Google properties	27,245	25,131
Google Network Members' properties	5,249	4,736
Google advertising	32,494	29,867
Google Cloud	2,100	3,007
Google other[1]	4,080	5,124
Google revenues	38,674	37,998
Other Bets revenues	162	148
Hedging gains	108	151
Total revenues	$38,944	$38,297
Total TAC	$7,238	$6,694
Number of employees	107,646	127,498

[1] YouTube non-advertising revenues are included in Google other revenues.

You can take all that information and combine it with both prior growth rates and estimates for future growth rates to determine your own assumptions. In this case I have an assumed earnings growth rate of 5% much lower than historically we've seen with Alphabet, and then in years two through five returning to a 15% growth rate. In this case I have a price earnings multiple of 25, as typically Google trades at a slight price during his multiple discounts, compared to Facebook. From these assumptions, my model assumes an ending price of 2087 dollars which would produce a 12% rate of return, assuming we could buy the stock at roughly 1184 dollars. Currently the stock is trading 25% above that fair valuation estimate meaning that there may be short-term downside risk of up to 20% in the stock if we should see a reversion to this estimated fair value. When comparing Google on Facebook, of the two at least right now, I think Facebook is arguably the better value. However, I do own both in my own portfolio and plan to continue to hold them for many years.

Model Results				
Dividend Yield at Sale:		0.00%	Current Dividend Yield:	0.00%
Sum of Reinvested Dividends:	0%	$0.00	Sum of Uninvested Dividends:	$0.00
Sale Price in 5 Yrs:	100%	$2,087.59	Sale Price in 10 Yrs:	$2,087.59
Total Value at Sale:	100%	$2,087.59	Total Cash Proceeds:	$2,087.59

		Projected Capital Gain/Loss After 5 Years	
Fair Valuation (at 12% RRR):	$1,184.56	At Fair Valuation:	76.23%
Current Price:	$1,482.76	At Current Price:	40.79%
Margin of Safety (%):	0%	Fair Valuation P/E:	26.1
Overvalued (%):	25%	Current P/E:	32.6
Upside to Fair Value (%):	0%		
Downside Risk (%):	-20%		

Year	EPS	Dividends	Share Price	Reinvested	P/E Multiple
Start	$45.47	$0.00	$1,184.56	$0.00	26.1

Next let's take a look at Microsoft. Microsoft has actually seen quite consistent results even throughout the recession and that is partly attributable to many companies moving up their timeline for their plans of digital transformation, which has accelerated the demand for Microsoft's enterprise software services.

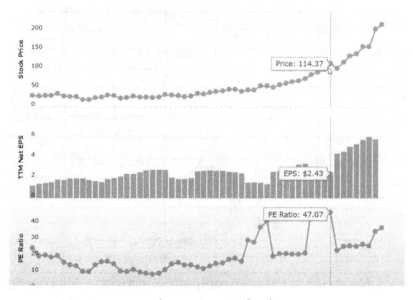

Most recently Microsoft has seen revenue growth of 13% and that has actually been quite consistent over the last several years and is likely expected to continue going forward. In this case I've modeled a consistent 13% growth in earnings over the next five years. Probably where there's most debate in modeling Microsoft is what is the right terminal priced earnings multiple. Taking a look at the long-term view of Microsoft stock price above their earnings in the middle and the price earnings ratio below, we can see that that price earnings ratio has increased from roughly around 10 in the early 2010s and Microsoft now is trading with a priced earnings ratio over 30. The spikes in price earnings ratio represent one-time impairments that occurred to earnings which aren't really representative of the true trend. Ignoring those spikes, you can still see that Microsoft's valuation multiple has increased steadily over the last decade. This valuation expansion cannot continue to infinity and there's a point where investors will say that's simply too expensive. However, what's really the right valuation multiple? Well, Microsoft back in the 2010s at a price earnings ratio of 10 was an incredible value, which didn't properly reflect the growth prospects for the company. A price to Earnings ratio around 24, fairly represents that but I can certainly see arguments for a higher price earnings multiple when you compare Microsoft to the multiples of many other SaaS companies. SaaS companies being companies providing software as a service typically under a subscription model and these companies have historically traded at very high price earnings multiples. Assuming a price earnings multiple of 24 which is what we'll look at to start with, we get an expected fair valuation price of $154. Compared to the current price of $216, the model is telling us that the stock is 40% overvalued to that fair value price or implies a roughly 30% downside from current levels. But if let's say based on your analysis that a proper price earnings multiple might be actually closer to 30 for Microsoft, then that downside risk starts to look a lot more reasonable compared to the current price, as the fair valuation has increased now to $192. This does however put a little bit more risk in your assumptions as you have to assume that Microsoft indeed does hit these 13% growth rates, but in addition to that those investors five years from now will be willing to pay 30 times earnings for Microsoft's earnings at that point. Those are just some things to keep in mind. Microsoft is a fantastic business and company, but the stock is arguably pretty expensive. In order to justify paying the current prices for Microsoft, you have to assume that investors will be willing to pay a relatively high multiple for the stock in five years. With the company executing as well as Microsoft, that is certainly possible, but it is something to consider.

Next, let's take a look at Apple and this is certainly again one of the most popular stocks out there, in addition to having some of the most popular products, Apple has generated significant returns for investors over the years. In this most recent quarter during the recession, Apple has been able to generate 11% revenue growth and earnings per share is up 18% compared to the quarter last year.

Apple Inc.

CONDENSED CONSOLIDATED STATEMENTS OF OPERATIONS (Unaudited)
(In millions, except number of shares which are reflected in thousands and per share amounts)

	Three Months Ended		Nine Months Ended	
	June 27, 2020	June 29, 2019	June 27, 2020	June 29, 2019
Net sales:				
Products	$ 46,529	$ 42,354	$ 170,598	$ 162,354
Services	13,156	11,455	39,219	33,780
Total net sales [1]	59,685	53,809	209,817	196,134

Much of this growth was attributable to strong iPhone sales, but their services segment is still growing quite quickly. Many people believe that the high growth in the service segment is arguably part of the future of Apple as an investment and is used as justification for why investors should be willing to pay a higher multiple for Apple than they have in the past. Taking a look at the price earnings multiple over Apple, which is the third bottom graph, you'll notice that Apple is currently trading at the highest priced earnings multiple, since the early days of the iPhone growth. There have been many periods over the last decade, specifically in 2011, 2013, 2015 and early 2016, and late 2008 where Apple has traded at multiples in the low teens. I.e., this being a price earnings multiple somewhere between 10 and 13. Now however Apple is trading at price earnings multiples two and a half to three times those cyclical lows. Are these price levels really justified, and can Apple maintain such a premium stock valuation? Those are going to have to be key questions you ask yourself when you're doing modeling for Apple.

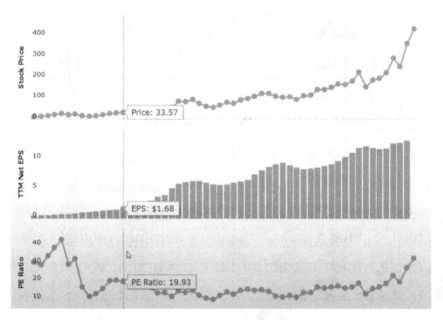

In this case Apple has seen recently quite strong growth in earnings per share so I've modeled that as 13% for the first two years, however I do think that we'll have to slow down which I've reflected as an 11% growth rate over the next three years following that. I think this is actually a relatively aggressive assumption because we have seen periods in the past where Apple has had no or even negative revenue growth, which is partly attributable to iPhone sales, which make up still a large component of revenue and have historically been somewhat cyclical. Add to that the fact that while Apple has been very shareholder friendly, giving back significant amounts of capital to investors in the form of dividends and particularly share buybacks, share buybacks at a price to earnings multiple above 30 will simply not be as effective in adding value to shareholders, as they were in the low teens. Really again it comes down to what is the proper multiple to pay for Apple stock. Apple's certainly a fantastic company so I think it deserves a premium multiple but is 30 plus really justified? In this case I've set it at 19, which will give us an example benchmark for what we're looking at in the model. In this case assuming the model assumptions are true, Apple is relatively significantly overvalued or at least expensive compared to our assumptions.

Model Results				
Dividend Yield at Sale:		0.33%	Current Dividend Yield:	0.19%
Sum of Reinvested Dividends:	2%	$7.49	Sum of Uninvested Dividends:	$6.05
Sale Price in 5 Yrs:	98%	$458.81	Sale Price in 10 Yrs:	$458.81
Total Value at Sale:	**100%**	**$466.29**	**Total Cash Proceeds:**	**$464.86**

			Projected Capital Gain/Loss After 5 Years	
Fair Valuation (at 12% RRR):		$264.59	At Fair Valuation:	73.40%
Current Price:		$435.75	At Current Price:	5.29%
Margin of Safety (%):		0%	Fair Valuation P/E:	20.1
Overvalued (%):		65%	Current P/E:	33.1
Upside to Fair Value (%):		0%		
Downside Risk (%):		-39%		

Year	EPS	Dividends	Share Price	Reinvested	P/E Multiple
Start	$13.15	$0.82	$264.59	$0.00	20.1

In this case we have a fair valuation of roughly 265 dollars, compared to the current price of $235 - meaning that if we were to see reversion back to this fair valuation based on our assumptions, it'd be a downside risk of roughly 39%. Another neat thing we can do is that we can actually estimate what the expected future returns would be for Apple investors at the current price, assuming that all our model assumptions hold true. The way we do this is we adjust the required rate of return, such that the modeled fare evaluation equals the current stock price. In this case with a little bit of trial and error, a 1.3 annualized rate of return is what investors would expect to get over the course of five years, assuming all these model assumptions hold true. While earnings have contributed to that expected return, almost just as much of return has been subtracted by that valuation multiple coming down over the course of those five years. If we see Apple trading at a price earnings ratio of 19 in five years, paying 437 dollars per share, this is prior to the four to one stock split, doesn't seem like a very attractive opportunity when you take into account both the risk and reward. You can certainly set your own assumptions which may get you to come to a different conclusion, but at least my view right now is that Apple is quite an expensive stock.

Speaking of expensive stocks, no discussion would be fully complete without bringing up Amazon. Amazon has been a significant beneficiary of the environment surrounding the recession.

Not only has it seen an explosion of growth within its north American retail segment with net sales up 43% and operating income up 37%, but international sales have seen significant growth as well with net sales up 38% year-over-year, and the segment reporting its first operating profit. In addition to this, AWS remains the dominant player in the Cloud space with sales up 29% and operating income up 58% over the last year.

Segment Results – AWS

Net Sales (MM)

$12,500

$8,381

Up 29% Y/Y

$10,808

Q2 2019 Q3 2019 Q4 2019 Q1 2020 Q2 2020

Operating Income (MM $5,000)

Up 58%Y/Y;
Up 54% F/X Adjusted

$3,357

$2,500 $2,121

Q2 2019 Q3 2019 Q4 2019 Q1 2020 Q2 2020

TTM Net Sales $40.0B

As the push towards accelerated digital transformation continues, this growth is likely to be strong going forward as well. Because of this such strong and robust growth that investors have been willing so far to pay such a high price for Amazon stock. Modeling with high growth rates can be challenging because even a small change in those high growth rate assumptions can make a fairly substantial difference on the ultimate stock fare evaluation price. In this case, I've assumed an annualized growth rate of 25% over each of those five years. Amazon's currently trading at a price earnings ratio of well over 100 when it's historically traded at around 80. In this case I might actually be making quite a conservative assumption, assuming Amazon will be trading at 50 price earnings multiple in five years, in which case based on that annualized 25% growth rate, the stock will be nearing 4,000 dollars in that time.

Model Results					
Dividend Yield at Sale:		0.00%	Current Dividend Yield:	0.00%	
Sum of Reinvested Dividends:	0%	$0.00	Sum of Uninvested Dividends:	$0.00	
Sale Price in 5 Yrs:	100%	$3,968.81	Sale Price in 10 Yrs:	$3,968.81	
Total Value at Sale:	100%	$3,968.81	Total Cash Proceeds:	$3,968.81	

		Projected Capital Gain/Loss After 5 Years	
Fair Valuation (at 12% RRR):	$2,252.01	At Fair Valuation:	76.23%
Current Price:	$3,111.89	At Current Price:	27.54%
Margin of Safety (%):	0%	Fair Valuation P/E:	86.6
Overvalued (%):	38%	Current P/E:	119.6
Upside to Fair Value (%):	0%		
Downside Risk (%):	-28%		

Year	EPS	Dividends	Share Price	Reinvested	P/E Multiple
Start	$26.01	$0.00	$2,252.01	$0.00	86.6

If all those model assumptions were true, this would get us to a fair valuation of roughly $2.252 which is about 28% lower than the current price of $3112. Given the very high growth rates and also expected high valuations for Amazon, this is what makes modeling the stock quite difficult. Given these circumstances Amazon is actually able to grow even faster than we've modeled in our expectations. For instance, say Amazon achieves a 35% growth in earnings over the next year and then 30% annually after that, well then, our fair value jumps quite significantly now just 9% less than the current price. If we assume that the price earnings ratio actually ends up at 65, well then, the expected price of Amazon in five years will be close to 6.500 dollars - meaning that if we actually bought Amazon today at its current price, we'd be buying at a 16% margin of safety or discount to its true fair value - assuming all our model assumptions are true. It's important in modeling and doing your valuation work that you don't model with an end result in mind. Doing so may influence your decisions in setting assumptions to try and end up with a predetermined result. Ideally you want to set your best estimate assumptions first and end up just seeing what the model results are. If they end up differing from your expectations significantly, well then that's a new insight you've gained. For across these five stocks, we've just looked at the base case valuation, but you can also build an unfavorable and favorable valuation case to get a range of estimates of a fair value to pay for each of these stocks and give you a sense of both the potential upside and downside case scenarios.

Chapter 2
Top 5 Stocks for
the Next 5 Years

When you're exploring and researching potential stocks to add to your portfolio, it can be a bit overwhelming given just the vast number of choices that you have. In this chapter will hopefully break that process down and make it a little bit less intimidating by taking a look at five specific stocks and discuss several investment considerations, including both the risks and opportunities for each stock over the next five years. The stocks we'll be looking at are Disney, Discover Financial Services, Cigna, Activision Blizzard, and Twitter. Let's jump into the first stock which is Disney. Disney is one of the largest media and entertainment companies in the world. They derive revenues from four segments media networks, parks experience and consumer products, studio entertainment and also their direct to consumer and an international segment. Of these four segments media and parks are definitely the largest of the two, making up the vast majority of both the revenue and operating earnings for the company. However, Disney stock has recently hit an all-time high with the announcement of their new direct to consumer service Disney Plus, which was launched to the public on November 12, 2019. Why this is a big deal on something to think about over the next several years when investing in Disney, is that Disney is pricing their new streaming service at a very competitive price point at $6.99 per month and under $6 per month if you choose the $70 per year option. Disney has a huge collection of Intellectual property with Disney Pixar, Marvel Star Wars and National Geographic recently acquired from Fox. A large portion of this content will be available to stream day 1 at launch for Disney Plus. At seven bucks per month this is a relatively compelling value given the amount of content that Disney can provide. Based on the aggressive price point, it doesn't look like Disney is trying to compete directly with Netflix as a complete alternative at this point. However, this could potentially change over time as they could bundle Disney Plus with other compelling content like ESPN and Hulu. Either way, we can get some insight into how these the likely impact financials from the commentary from their CFO. Specifically, they're expecting roughly sixty to ninety million subscribers about a third of them from the US and the rest international. To support the new streaming service, Disney will also be investing in original content, similar to what Netflix is doing right now spending about 1 billion per year 2022 about 2.5 billion in 2024. It's important for Disney investors to note that while the streaming service is just getting off the ground and growing, the segment will be operating at a loss in the near-term. Those losses are expected to peak somewhere in the next one to three years, and Disney won't expect the service to be profitable until about 2024. Given the aggressive pricing and growth strategy for Disney, it doesn't come as too much of a surprise for me to see the significant price action over the two days. Prior to this Disney was trading at roughly fifteen to sixteen prices to earnings multiple, now post Disney Plus we've seen that multiple shoots up to eighteen. Historically speaking this level valuation is still within normal trading ranges for Disney, but investors should note that it will take some time for that increase in revenue from Disney Plus to translate to the bottom line with an increased profitability. Overall, Disney has a wide economic moat and a clear avenue for growth going forward. With that in mind new investors may want to keep an eye on valuation multiples, as reversions back to the lower historical range might be potential buying opportunities for Disney.

The next stock we are going to look at is Discover Financial Services. When it comes to credit card issuers and payment networks, there are four big players in the US; Visa, Mastercard, American Express and Discover. By purchase volume Visa is the largest followed by Mastercard, American Express and then at the bottom; Discover. You can look at this in a couple of ways; one is that Visa and Mastercard both certainly have a stronger competitive position, at least in terms of the economic moat of their wide payment networks. On the other hand, that's at least partially priced in as Visa and Mastercard are trading at much higher price to earnings multiples, compared to Discover, so much more of the price of the stock of Mastercard and Visa is based on the expectations of continued high rates of future growth. For Discover on the other hand much of the stock prices based on current earnings, so any future growth beyond expectations would be additional upside to Discover stock. Part of the reason why Discover and also to an extent American Express are trading at lower valuation multiples, is because as a company they have a higher degree of risk than the business models of Mastercard and Visa. Unlike Discover and American Express, Visa and Mastercard don't actually issue credit card debt. They simply operate their payment network in which banks then issue credit cards in their name. Because Visa and Mastercard get paid based on a percentage of each transaction that goes through on their payment network, they don't have any default risks that could potentially occur during economic recessions, where American Express into a greater extent Discover could potentially see defaults on those loans. Looking at discovers credit performance trends, we can start to see some of that trend actually already starting to occur. Both the net charge off rates and delinquency rates have been gradually increasing over the last three years for their book of loans. Net charge off rates being the amount of discovers loans that likely aren't going to be paid back. This is gradually increased from about

2% three years ago to now roughly 3%. Having 3% of your loans not being paid back doesn't seem like a good thing, however if you look at the average interest rate that Discover is earning on their loan balances, they were charging on average roughly 12.5% interest - meaning by no means is this an unprofitable book of business, even after considering the modestly increasing that charge-off rates. The big question is where will these net charge-off rates be during periods of economic stress? It's hard to predict exactly where it'll be long term, but at least for the short-term Discover expects for this modest trend to continue. In 2019 they expect that charged-off rate to increase roughly to 3.2 to 3.4%. Visa and Mastercard also not completely immune to recessions either, as that will likely see a decrease in payment volumes, as well as likely a decrease in valuation multiple, so that's one thing to consider for investing Discover. Discover off to make sure they're managing their book of loans properly, and not reduce their loan issuing standards in hope of revenue growth. So far, they've been able to do that relatively well, growing their book of loans, while maintaining their standards for credit quality. Another thing to note we

Discover is that they have a very friendly shareholder capital allocation plan. Over the last five years they've consistently bought back company's stock and have decreased the share count by roughly 30% over the last five years. This has allowed them to grow earnings per share quite significantly, despite revenue growth remaining relatively modest. Overall, Discover doesn't have quite as a significant economic compared to Visa or Mastercard with much wider payment networks, it does come with more attractive current valuations as well as a higher dividend yield. Investors looking for exposure to financials and credit services might consider Discover as an investment, so long as they're aware of the potential risk that an economic recession could bring and the impact to both Discover's loan business and the stock price.

The next stock we are going to look at is Cigna. Cigna is a global health services company that provides health insurance and other supplementary products to individuals, families, and businesses. In the healthcare space they're one of the mid side health insurers, and much smaller at least compared to the larger United Health Group. Despite this, Cigna has shown an impressive strong track record of growth through a dynamic and changing health care market. Recently though Cigna stock and the stock of many other health care companies have been under pressure over concerns about uncertainty of future health care regulation, specifically surrounding the price of prescription drugs. Cigna's recent purchase of pharmacy benefit manager Express Scripts has made their stock particularly sensitive to these concerns. Despite these short-term concerns, Cigna looks to be in a position to continue its strong growth over the next five years. They expect to roughly double their 2017 earnings per share by 2021. The way they plan to do this is to continue expanding their four core segments, each with a strategic plan for growth. One of the things that Cigna does well and makes it stand out relative to other health insurers, is that they have a strategic focus on aligning incentives, both between customers, clients, and health care providers. Effectively instead of just reimbursing medical expenses whenever a patient gets sick. Cigna works with employers to design plans that are meant to keep its employees healthier. In addition to this, Cigna has several contracts with health care providers, where instead of simply reimbursing doctors and physicians based on the number of services they provide, their reimbursement is based on patient health outcomes. This way the financial incentive of doctors is more aligned with customers and the insurer, which at the end of the day, ultimately enables better care at a lower cost. From a valuation perspective Cigna is trading at a discount relative to peers and the general market, however this is to be expected, given that they did complete a large acquisition with Express Scripts, and typically an acquiring company post-acquisition sees a decline in their valuation because the premium they paid to the acquired company has to be absorbed by the current shareholders. Given the recent stock price, this appears to be priced in for the most part. Investors looking to gain exposure to the healthcare space specifically through health insurers, might consider Cigna as a potential option. Do note that they pay a nominal penny per quarter dividend, so the majority of the returns to expect from the stock will be in the form of capital appreciation. Overall, the company has strong headwinds behind it with an aging US population and has a strong management team that has shown consistent growth over the years. But investors should be aware of the uncertainty around potential health care regulation, which could continue to compress multiples for the stock for some time. Additionally, Cigna will need to deleverage their balance sheet after the Express Scripts merger, something that will take a higher priority in terms of capital allocation.

Next stock we are going to take a look at is Activision Blizzard. This is a stock had a significant price of run-up we saw in 2017 in the first half of 2018, only to see a resetting of expectations in the latter half of 2018, where the stock declined over 50%. Activision Blizzard is a video game publishing company, and they have several well-established franchises. They have three main operating segments, Activision, Blizzard, and King digital. Activision is best known for their Call of Duty franchise, which is one of the best-selling console franchises worldwide. Blizzard Entertainment includes franchises like Overwatch, Hearthstone and World of Warcraft. King Digital is focused on mobile gaming and has one of the highest grossing US. apps and mobile app stores with Candy Crush Saga, part of the Candy Crush franchise. Part of the reason why Activision saw such a strong price run-up in 2017 was due to the success of their new release Overwatch in the prior year, as well as seen significant multiple expansion in the stock. At its peak, Activision was trading at what some would consider nosebleed valuation levels, at price turning multiples well in excess of 40. Today while still above market averages at 23 price-to-earnings - the stock appears to be at more reasonable valuation levels. Question is is this a fair price today considering the expected growth for Activision going forward? One thing worth noting for investors in Activision Blizzard is that many of the franchises that the company owned are relatively mature franchises. Call of Duty and World of Warcraft have been around for over a decade and while Activision did see an all-time record in operating income from the release of Black Ops 4, World of Warcraft subscribers are continuing to gradually decline over time. With the rise in popularity of free-to-play titles like Fortnite and Apex Legends, these titles might pressure the sales of Activision Blizzard's more mature franchises in the future. If this is the case, Activision's growth might be less than what investors are currently expecting. Right now, the company's growth strategy is to focus on product development within those core franchises. In addition, they're cutting costs and reducing admin expenses and removing funding from underperforming initiatives, in addition to trying to scale commercial opportunities throughout the business. Overall, in the near term it's a transition period for the company. Absent any new hit game releases Activision Blizzard will be more heavily reliant on their mature franchises. It's certainly possible they may release several new popular games over the next five years or so, but the uncertainty surrounding the commercial success of those games and the longevity of how long they can last before consumers move on to the next big thing and compare that into the cost of development, it adds an additional layer of uncertainty surrounding the stock. Over the last past eight years or so, Activision stock has seen a period of significant growth, however it's worth knowing that when that period of growth started roughly from 2011 to 2013, Activision was trading at a price multiple between 10 and 15, which is over 30% to 50% lower than where it stands today. A reversion back to those multiples from prices today would mean the stock would likely need to trade below $30 per share. A 30% drop might seem hard to imagine after already seeing a 50% drop just in last year, this is a scenario I consider relatively possible in the context of a recession or a period of slower economic growth. That isn't necessarily guaranteed, and Activision may retain a higher multiple, but it is something for investors to keep in mind as a possibility. Overall, for investors interested investing in the chapter game space, Activision Blizzard is a well-established player, but I usually recommend taking valuations into consideration when buying the stock and if a shareholder don't be afraid to sell if you see valuations running up beyond expectations like they did in 2018.

The final stock in this chapter I want to take a look at is Twitter. If you were an initial investor in Twitter at IPO, you probably aren't too happy with how the investment turned out, as Twitter is still below its price on IPO day. However, that was over seven years ago and now the company's a little more established and is actually profitable at this point.

What's the investment opportunity with Twitter and what are the risks? Well, as a social media company, Twitter effectively monetizes attention through advertisements on their site and platform. One of the core metrics related to this revenue generation is their monetizable daily active usage. Daily users of social media platforms are important because they are the most active users on the platform and drive the largest amount of ad revenue per user. The year-over-year growth rate in daily active usage is actually in decline for Twitter at 12% at the end of 2019 now down to 9% at the end of 2020. For monthly active users or users that access the platform at least once a month, that is actually down year-over-year. This is indicating that the overall user base for Twitter is in decline, even if it is modest. I suppose they didn't particularly want to highlight this as they did not add the year-over-year growth percentage, but we can calculate that on our own and at the end of 2019, monthly active usage was down roughly 3% from a year ago. Despite this Twitter has been able to increase their revenue through increases in app prices, as well as increases in revenues from data licensing. While this increase in revenue is positive there are a few potential risks worth pointing out with twitter at least compared to other social media appears like Facebook. Compared to Facebook, Twitter users have lower rates of user engagement, which translates to lower ad revenue per user. Facebook with their Facebook and Instagram apps are able to more effectively monetize their user base and also keep engagement levels much higher. In addition to that, Facebook is showing more robust levels of user growth even if they are slowing, compared to Twitter who's seen declines in monthly active usage. This would be less of an issue from an investment standpoint if Twitter was trading at a significant discount to Facebook, however relative to earnings both Twitter and Facebook are trading at roughly 22 to 24 times earnings. While Facebook has a very wide economic moat with its strong network effect, Twitter hasn't been able to demonstrate an economic moat over the past five years and that's something I think makes the company a bit more vulnerable during a period of recession. During the recession, advertising spending generally gets cut very heavily. When this happens, all social media companies will likely see a decrease in both revenue and earnings. However, for the remaining advertising budget that is left for online spending, I would expect the majority of that will go to Facebook, rather than Twitter, as Facebook represents a higher return on investment for advertisers, compared to a service like Twitter. Given this and also the fact that the majority of the stock price is supported by the expectation of continued higher rates of growth, I think Twitter stock has the potential to continue to be volatile. Given this, investors potentially considering the stock, might want to opt for a larger margin of safety before making their initial purchase. I don't think the company is in any financial trouble, given the high amount of cash per share and relatively manageable levels of debt, I do think the higher levels of growth that are baked into expectations right now leave material downside for the stock if those don't pan out. If I were forced to choose a social media company to invest in right now, I would likely pick Facebook over Twitter, given the larger economic moat and likely more resilient earnings during poor economic conditions. Though at a lower stock price, Twitter might look compelling for a short-term investment.

Chapter 3
Top 5 Stocks to Buy for Long Term Returns

In this chapter I'll be sharing five of my favorite stocks all of which I have owned that can help generate long-term returns for your portfolio year after year. Hopefully regardless of your portfolio and goals you can find a useful idea to consider for future investment. The first is one of those consistent growing value stocks and personally one of my favorites and it's AutoZone, ticker symbol AZO. AutoZone is primarily a US-based retailer and distributes automotive replacement parts and accessories, so through its retail network it provides customers a wide range of products to complete all their auto repair maintenance and improvement projects. As of august 2020 they operated nearly 5,900 stores in the us as well as 621 stores in Mexico and 43 in Brazil. As of January 2020, AutoZone is trading at a 28-billion-dollar market cap and reported $70 of earnings per share over the last 12 months. There are a lot of things to like about AutoZone particularly from a shareholder perspective which is why I consider them an "A Tier" quality stock. First off, their management team is excellent with a long-term focus on both business growth and shareholder returns. The CEO William Rhodes has been leading the company since he assumed that role back in 2005. However, even prior to that he'd been working at various executive roles within AutoZone since 1994. The rest of the executive management team is just as seasoned and experienced, and the results show that they know what they're doing. As of January 2020, AutoZone stock is 14 times higher than it was when Rhoads took over in 2005, and if you were fortunate enough to invest $10,000 on the first day of AutoZone's IPO back in April 1991, well that amount would have grown to 1.7 million dollars by the start of 2020. How did they do it and achieve such phenomenal returns for shareholders? Well, the secret sauce has to do in part with management's relentless focus on maintaining a high ROIC - return on invested capital. This makes sure any new capital added to the business is compounding at a high rate of return, accelerating future growth in earnings per share. This is such an important metric for AutoZone that part of executive pay is actually tied to maintaining these high ROC targets. This is something that's actually very rare among S&P 500 companies. Tied to this strategy is the fact that AutoZone has been exceptionally efficient at repurchasing its shares which has been its primary avenue for returning excess capital to shareholders. On the business side an additional benefit of AutoZone is that it typically performs well both during periods of economic expansion as well as contraction. That is because as an auto repair retailer their business primarily depends on two factors; one is the total miles driven in the US, and two; the average age of those vehicles in use. As the economy is strong, people tend to drive more but as the economy slows down, the average age of used vehicles tends to increase. There are a few risks that are worth mentioning. One is that AutoZone already now has a large network of stores so new store openings will be at a slower pace than in the past. Second, AutoZone uses leverage on their balance sheet to optimize return to shareholder by buying back shares using cheap debt. If financing costs change in the future and AutoZone is required to pay a higher rate of interest for that debt, it could impact future buybacks. A more long-term potential risk is with the growth of electric vehicles in the future, it's possible that there may be less need and or demand for traditional auto repair and maintenance parts. Though personally I think that if electric vehicles were to grow significantly in terms of a percent of total US vehicles, AutoZone would likely have time to adapt to this new market. Overall, I'm a big fan of AutoZone stock own it in my portfolio and typically try to add when the price earnings ratio is attractive; below 15.

The second quality stock that would be great for a long-term portfolio is Centene Corporation, ticker symbol CNC. Centene Corporation provides health care programs and services to underinsured and uninsured individuals in the United States. Centene is the number one provider of managed Medicaid services and also is increasing market share in the fast-growing Medicare advantage segment. They've compounded earnings per share 19% annualized since their IPO in 2005 and at even higher rates looking back over the last five years. Historically Centene has been relatively acquisitive in terms of purchasing other companies to help generate more earnings over time. One of those recent purchases was their well care acquisition, which may cause Centene to see slightly lower rates of earnings growth for the near future, though over the long term they're still targeting roughly 10% organic revenue growth, which should translate to continued strong growth earnings per share in the future. In terms of revenue, Centene has three rough segments: managed Medicaid, commercial and Medicare. Medicaid provides health insurance for those below the Federal poverty limit and by using Centene's managed Medicaid program enrollees can get preventative care as well as a primary care physician at lower cost than a traditional Medicaid plan. Additionally, the total Medicaid market is expected to grow by roughly 5 to 6% over the next decade, which should directly help Centene grow as they are the leader in the Medicaid space. The commercial business isn't broken out, but it primarily consists of state-driven marketplace plans, which are mandated by the affordable care act. The final segment Medicare is the most profitable on a per member basis, as retirees typically require the most complex care. Upon turning 65 in the US retirees are given several options into how to receive Medicare insurance going forward. One of those options is purchasing a Medicare advantage plan, which is offered by private insurers including Centene. For some retirees these plans have the potential to offer more benefits at lower cost than the traditional Medicare option. In fact, Medicare advantage plans are gaining popularity and it's expected that roughly 40% to 45% of seniors will be selecting one of these plants by 2025 with that percentage potentially increasing to 70% by 2040. Currently about 35% of seniors select a Medicare advantage plan. There are certainly some risks with Centene. For one, they are health insurers, so they are taking on the risk of the people that they insure. For instance, when Centene wins new state managed Medicare business, initial margins might typically be low as those enrollees may have catch-up health care expenses and needs that they will initially use. This can cause higher upfront expenses for Centene as they process and reimburse those health care expenditures, but then later on the expenses tend to normalize over time. This can cause some volatility around earnings, which potentially could be a buying opportunity if the market reacts unfavorably. Additionally, Centene has been acquisitive by nature, so if they overpay for a potential future acquisition that could be a drag on earnings in the future. Finally, there's always regulatory and legislative risk when you're talking about health care insurers. This was something that compressed price earnings multiples for all health insurers from 2008 to 2012, prior to the affordable care act being finalized. If there's potential investor uncertainty surrounding changes to future legislation, this could also put some compression on those multiples again in the future. Overall Centene is an excellent company and can also be an attractive stock. There have been periods in time when Centene is trading at or below 14 times earnings and paying 14 times earnings for a company that's growing 10% annualized earnings per share over the next three to five years is something that's hard to find in today's markets. Overall, it's a stock I'm happy to own in my portfolio for the long term.

Next is a defensive blue-chip company I hold in my portfolio and that is Kroger, ticker symbol KR. Kroger operates the largest pure food retailer in the

United States. While the largest player in the us grocery market is Walmart, Kroger is sitting strong in that second place. Compared to the previous two stocks, Kroger is what I would consider a slow grower it would probably fall in my "B Tier" of quality stocks on my watch list, but still one that can be beneficial for its defensive properties. Back in March of 2020 when many stocks were falling 20% or 30%, Kroger stock was actually up over that period in time. Additionally, Kroger was one of the few stocks to be up in 2008 during the financial crisis. The reason for this is relatively simple; everyone needs to eat. It's easy to delay purchasing a new car but it's much harder to delay purchasing groceries. Because of this Kroger benefits from relatively stable revenues over time and more recently has benefited from an increase in at-home food spending. As of March 2020, they operated over 2750 stores across the US under various names. Additionally, they have significant and growing sales from their private label brands including Simply Truth - one of the top selling organic brands in the US. Kroger has done a fairly good job of managing expenses, while also making investments for the future. Most stores have expanded their online grocery fulfillment capabilities, which allow some shoppers a more convenient experience. From a valuation perspective, Kroger is quite profitable and trading at relatively low-price earnings ratios. I purchased my stock in Kroger a little under 27 dollars per share, and Berkshire Hathaway is actually invested in Kroger as well around 28 to 29 dollars per share. When it comes to groceries and food retail, one of the biggest risks is competition. Food retail is a very low margin business. Kroger doesn't make a lot of money on the items they sell, but they make up for it in volume. If competitors over time start to eat away at Kroger's market share, that could hurt future profitability. Additionally, if Kroger potentially makes poor investments or poor capital allocation decisions, potentially regarding investment in online fulfilment or other areas, that potential malinvestment could also be a drag on future performance. Overall, I like Kroger as a defensive holding in a portfolio. It is a very suitable option for investors looking for a stable dividend, as well as a company that experiences nice and slow but steady growth. This could potentially also be used as a bond proxy stock, replacing a bond component of your portfolio, if you fully understand and are aware of the risks.

Finally, we have our emerging growth company - a bit higher risk but potential for higher reward as well. This company is called Bandwidth, ticker symbol BAND. Bandwidth's business is a communication platform as a service. They own nationwide voice messaging and 9-1-1 networks. These networks like the one Bandwidth owns allow other companies to communicate with customers in a systematic way through text messaging and other mobile devices. The other large player in this space is Twilio. Bandwidth is marketing themselves as a smarter and cheaper alternative. Some companies have certainly appreciated this approach including large brands such as Google, Microsoft and Zoom. For instance, Google uses Bandwidth's API network to manage their Google voice systems. Let's say you make a call or text from Google voice on your computer that'll be routed through Bandwidth's networks to whoever you're calling on their mobile device. In an increasingly digital economy, Bandwidth has recently seen accelerating growth. For instance, in the third quarter of 2020, they saw 40%

revenue growth compared to the quarter the year before. In addition to this, they boast a dollar based net retention rate of 131%. What this means is that on average the customers that were with Bandwidth last year, are purchasing 36% more with them this year. Having a dollar based net retention rate above 100%, can really accelerate growth for a fast-growing company, because not only are you adding on new customers to your existing customer base, but your previous cohort of customers are purchasing more with you as well. An additional potential benefit is that Bandwidth is still relatively small and under followed. Currently the market capitalization is under 4 billion which for fast growing tech stocks is quite small, considering the valuation of some other companies. For those with a long-term mindset and can stomach some intermediate-term volatility, fast-growing companies like Bandwidth could provide high potential return. That being said, don't be surprised at all by price drawdowns of 30, 40 or even 50% or more. While that may seem extreme, these price fluctuations are relatively typical among stocks with high expected growth potential. This is because the underlying valuation of these stocks can vary dramatically based on the assumptions, analysts and investors are using for that assumed growth rate over time. This can be both a risk and opportunity. Risk being if you purchase at a high valuation, then you may be sacrificing the potential upside return, as much of that is already priced into the stock. On the flip side, if you buy after a significant price decline, you're allowing yourself more upside potential if growth re-accelerates and less downside risk if it doesn't.

As for risks aside from valuation, one of the biggest ones would be competition with Twilio, which is the larger player in this market. While Bandwidth is succeeding in growing its customer base and sales, if they're trying to take customers away from Twilio, they may have to discount their margins in order to get that sale. This can increase revenue growth but then could make it a bit longer for the company to scale back into profitability. Generally, for emerging growth companies, I would label this as a more speculative growth stock as a component of a total portfolio. As part of your own risk management, you might have a rule not to invest more than say 5% or 10 % of your portfolio in these more speculative securities. These types of guidelines can help manage the risk in your portfolio, while still leaving you exposed to the potential upside of these fast-growing companies. Those are five of some of my favorite stocks to buy as long-term stock holdings. I currently have all five in my portfolio and will likely look to add to these positions in the future over time.

Chapter 4
Top 3 Stocks Under $5

In this chapter we're going to be talking about 3 stocks under $5 per share for long term investing. Before reading to my picks, I want to quickly cover what I believe is one of the most useful lessons that I've ever learned related to the stock market or investing in general, which is your corresponding risk and reward associated with different investments. Cash is certainty. That means your money is not really growing. It means it's not going away. It's just sitting there although it is going away due to inflation, but it is the most certain asset that people want is cash during times of uncertainty. Then you have Bonds which have a little bit of upside and a little bit of risk, but really not much at all there. So, I don't really invest in bonds whatsoever. After that we have Blue Chip stocks which is where the majority of my money is. These stocks have minimal risk and a little bit of upside, but not tons that we can speak of. Then we have Mid Cap growth and then Small Cap growth, and then we have Startups as well as Angel Investments. The whole point is that you want to understand based on the type of return that you may be looking for, what type of downside risk you may be exposing yourself to. Because most people out there would agree that they want to be this far up the reward spectrum as far as the upside from an investment. But what they don't realize is that in order to have this much upside, you have to have a lot of downsides too. The majority of my money is in blue chip stocks in my M1 Finance dividend stock portfolio. And I have a very small amount of money in small cap growth. What we're specifically talking about in this chapter are those small cap growth stocks under $5 per share that I've been purchasing in 2021. I am personally not putting my life savings into small cap stocks, and I certainly would not recommend it. Most financial experts would not. In this era where we're seeing a lot of people making these Yolo bets where they go all in on stocks. At the end of the day, it's up to you whether or not you invest in a stock you have to do your own research, but I wanted you to have a general idea of how much money I'm putting into these stocks. It's less than 10% of my total investment portfolio involved in these small cap growth stocks. Since there is more risk, there is potentially a lot more upside with these small cap stocks. That is why I have personally decided to purchase shares of these companies.

Number one on the list is the Very Good Food Company. It trades under the symbol VRYYF if you're here in the United States. They had a $339 million Market Cap in Canadian, hence they were a Small Cap stock. Since they are a Canadian company, they trade on the over-the-counter markets. Very Good Food Company is a plant-based food technology company that designs, develops, produces, distributes, and sells plant-based meats in the United States and Canada. They're offering their products via wholesale as well as e-commerce. The whole reason why I got involved with this company in the first place is because of a general paradigm shift going on with society, surrounding the consumption of animal products. A lot of people have been adopting vegetarian or vegan practices prior to this, but I become more vegan oriented in 2021 primarily due to a few documentaries I watched recently. If you haven't seen them, yet I would highly recommend checking them out. Number one is called Seaspiracy on Netflix - all about the terrible things we're doing to our oceans. Number two is called Cowspiracy. In a nutshell, what these documentaries have shown us is that it's literally impossible for us to continue eating the amount of animal product that we are. Not to mention we're also seeing a lot of mainstream acceptance and adoption of these larger meatless brands, for example the Impossible Breakfast Sandwich is now available at a lot of Starbucks locations and the Beyond Sausage Sandwich at Dunkin' Donuts. Thus, it's a really good time for this meatless entrance because it's essentially a mega trend behind them, which is this mainstream meatless adoption where people are really giving these meatless options a fair shot. Very Good Food Company is committed to expanding its suite of products beyond the butcher block with its eye ultimately on replacing animal products with nutritious and delicious plant-based options. Very Good Food Companies clean ingredient deck is what sets them apart from the competition, offering high quality artisanal style products with whole ingredients. Based on their annual report is they've had explosive growth from 2019 to 2020. E-commerce sales went from about 225,000 to over $3.3 million in 2020. One thing that has me excited in particular about this stock is regarding their eCommerce segment. As of December 31st, 2020, the company had over 800 active subscribers across Canada and in the US with new subscribers joining every day. The company currently has over 2000 active subscribers. That is pretty fast growth in the very short term. I always like these subscription-type businesses because this becomes a predictable stream of revenue for this company. On the wholesale side they work with about 1300 retail distribution points in Canada across 275 different stores, and we also saw a lot of growth here from 2019 to 2020 in terms of wholesale revenue. However, we are not talking about very big numbers here because this is a small up and coming company. The third segment of their business is the Butcher Shop & Restaurant Flagship Store. This is basically their test kitchen for trying new products, as well as a branding and marketing tool for themselves. They're also opening a second flagship store in Vancouver British Columbia, Mount Pleasant in quarter four of 2021, which is exciting as well. One of the things that I like in particular about this company is the fact that it's really not that expensive. They actually mailed me a ton of different samples of their products. They are 100% delicious and I would highly recommend them if you can get your hands on them, and we'll explain why that is later on. They essentially sell items individually or you can buy different meal kits, and you can get a plant-based meat kit here that makes 28 meals for just $99 US or there's a 13-meal box that's going to run you just $50. The idea behind their food products is that the whole food artisanal ingredients are designed by a top chef. Flavor comes first and it is healthier ingredients with a better taste profile. One of their biggest announcements comes from their cheese segment because they just recently acquired a brand called the Cultured Nut, and they're relaunching the Very Good Cheese Company. By quarter three of 2021, they hope to be selling Bold Cheddah, regular Cheddah Dell'ish, Gouda, and pepper Jack vegan cheeses which I am honestly very excited about trying myself. I try to keep my dairy intake to a minimal just for, phlegm reasons, but I am all about the vegan cheese and super excited to try this out myself. It's also another business that they can go after here, not just the meatless market but the dairy free cheese market. A lot of people are considering these animal free options, so there is a mega trend that I believe is present behind this company which should give them good growth Prospects in the future. As far as competitors go there's about five companies worth discussing here. You may notice that most of these companies are smaller, and that is because this is a new and emerging industry. The Very Good Food Company is well positioned to be a market leader, based on their investment in the actual taste of the product. The reviews speak for themselves, and I think they just have a better tasting product compared to what Beyond Meat is offering, and I've never personally tried Tattooed Chef, but at some point, I will definitely be trying them out as well. But if we compare them to their peers, Beyond Meat is valued at $6.75 billion, Tattooed Chef comes as 1.4. The Very Good Food Company is being valued at around $340 million, which is substantially less than the valuations of Beyond Meat as well as Tattooed Chef. If they are able to continue growing revenue and as the production comes online and they have more production available, this company could do extremely well going forward, which should hopefully translate into a larger market valuation and a higher share price, up there with the likes of Beyond Meat and Tattooed Chef. Other than that, there's two other stocks, with similar sizes to these companies that is Burcon, NutraScience with a $390 million Market Cap and then Layered Super Foods with a $310 million Market Cap. Since the company went public, they had a run-up to around $650 or $700 per share, but they've actually sold off substantially over the last six months. The idea behind this is many investors including me, seek to buy the dip. But the issue you can run into with that is it's impossible to tell where the bottom is. I would recommend the strategy of dollar cost averaging. So, rather than dumping all of your money in at once, you would be investing a little bit over a longer period of time. That way, if that price continues to move lower as it has in the past, you can lower your cost basis by purchasing more shares. If we compare the financials here of the Very Good Food Company with Beyond Meat, we can see that 2020 revenue for Beyond Meat was $406.8 million, while 2020 revenue for Very Good Food Company was just bullet $4.6 million.

	Beyond Meat	VERY GOOD Food Co.
2020 Revenue	$406.8m	$4.6m
Market Cap (USD)	$6,750,000,000	$340,000,000
YOY Revenue Growth	36.6%	364%

Roughly 100th of the revenue for Beyond Meat. If we look at the market caps for these companies, however this makes a lot of sense. The market is valuing Beyond Meat 6.75 billion US dollars, while Very Good Food Company is worth 340 million dollars. However, what gets me excited is the bottom row there talking about year over year revenue growth, year over year Beyond Meat only grew revenue by 36.6% last year whereas Very Good Food Company grew their revenue by an astounding 364%. We have two very different stocks; Very Good Food Company is still in that hyper growth mode, where if they're doing well, maybe their share price can go up very quickly if they can scale up revenue. Whereas with Beyond Meat, their growth is slowing down as they are becoming a larger and larger company. I would expect to see stronger growth numbers coming out from Very Good Food Company versus Beyond Meat just based on the size of these companies and where they are at as far as getting mainstream adoption for their products. The next thing I want to cover here is some details from their most recent earnings report. In particular, it is this paragraph about increasing production.

"As we continue to see increased market demand for our unique product portfolio, now consisting of 14 plus plant-based products, we are pleased to report that we are well positioned to reach our new level of growth for Very Good in 2021. We are on track with the rollout of our new production facility in Vancouver, providing us with a substantial growth opportunity to increase production capacity by 2690% with 37 million pounds of annualized product in 2021."

That is the main reason why I'm so excited about this company, is they're increasing production by an astronomical level which should allow them to begin filling orders. One of the problems this company is having right now is the fact that, they can't even keep up with the existing orders on their website because of the amount of interest in their product, and they just don't have the scale yet to produce enough for the demand. Once that production facility comes online, that should allow them to have more than enough product to meet that demand and grow revenue. As far as the new surrounding this company here are a couple of recent headlines. First of all, the Very Good Food Company has announced a retail distribution partnership with UNFI in the United States to give them a better foothold in this market. There's also a news article there about the increase of their production by over 2500% at their new facility, as well as their partnership with Green Spoon Sales to accelerate US retail growth. They're not going at it alone here; they're making strategic partnerships in the United States in order to expand and grow and get customers in the US market as they have more production. The main point we're getting at here is that production is increasing very shortly by over 2500%, which should substantially help this company with keeping up with demand for their products, as well as the new ones that they are launching such as the Very Good Cheese brand, which is being relaunched. I've been buying shares and dollar cost averaging and I plan on continuing to do so with the money that I personally choose to allocate towards these smaller cap growth stocks.

Number two on my list is Genius Brands, trading under symbol, GNUS. This is a US listed company trading on the NASDAQ. The good news is you can purchase this stock on any investing app out there that allows you to trade New York Stock Exchange and NASDAQ stocks. $462 million market cap so definitely small cap. Genius Brands is a content and brand management company that creates and licenses children's content. They licensed shows to Netflix, Amazon Prime, Nickelodeon, and more, and they also launched a 100% free Kartoon Channel App which absolutely slaps. They have over 6,000 reviews and a five-star rating. On top of that, they also control the Stan Lee brand, and there's a lot of opportunity there that I could see. First of all, I just wanted to explain the mission statement behind this company because it's a bit different than other companies out there. Essentially Genius Brands has the goal of delivering content with a purpose for toddlers and teens to provide a rich environment for entertainment as well as learning. This media company is not just making garbage cartoons, they're looking to create content with a purpose that's actually teaching children strong values. Warren Buffet also has a show with Genius Brands that we'll talk about in a little bit. The biggest show in the pipeline right now is "Shaq's Garage", starring none other than Shaquille O'Neal. That show is still in production. Llama Llama is starring on Netflix. That is a show that they are involved with. Then the biggest show released recently was "Stan Lee's Superhero Kindergarten" starring Arnold Schwarzenegger. That is available now for streaming on YouTube as well as the Kartoon Channel. It's also one of those children's shows that adults enjoy as well with a lot of funny jokes from Arnold Schwarzenegger's movie passed in different involvements. It's a really cool show for both kids and adults. They're clearly trying to make content that's not just for children, which should really help them in growing use of this app. "Rainbow Rangers" is one of their larger shows as well. It's over on Netflix as well as Nickelodeon. This has been their pilot show or one of the biggest ones that they had been working on prior to the release of "Stan Lee's Superhero Kindergarten". To name a couple of other shows; they have a show called "SpacePOP" featuring on YouTube. They have "Baby Genius" which is more of a children's show, and then "Thomas Edison's Secret Lab" which is a STEM-based learning show with over 50 episodes. Then of course, Warren Buffet's "Secret Millionaires Club" created with and starring iconic investor, Warren Buffet including special guests, Jay-Z, Bill Gates, and Shaquille O'Neil. The number of names that this company is involved with is honestly ridiculous and that is one of the reasons why I like this stock is because of the relationships that Andy Heyward, the CEO has built with a lot of very influential people in this world. In addition to that, they have an up-and-coming show called "Martha & Friends" starring Martha Stewart. The other two there, Gisele and the Green Team that is something I would imagine is related to the Stan Lee deal. And then "Stan Lee's Mighty 7". A lot of cool stuff in the pipeline here and what Genius Brands is doing right now, is they're not focused on revenue, they're not focused on making money, they're focused on building a massive user-base for their free app, purchasing up really high-quality media assets in this space, and in addition, they are investing a lot of their money into original content for their own platform as well as other streaming platforms out there. Let's talk a bit more about the Stanley name here and how that relates to Genius Brands. Genius Brands has in their possession over 100 original unexploited properties, created by the legendary Stan Lee whose Marvel universe has driven over $41 billion in box office alone at Marvel. That is very interesting about this company is the fact that they have the control of the Stan Lee name as well as over 100 unexploited properties that they will be able to roll out on their Kartoon Channel. In terms of the distribution that this company has, they're already pretty much everywhere. You can get them on YouTube, Roku, Apple TV, Amazon Prime Video, Dish, Sling and then a bunch of other ones that I haven't even heard of. That list is growing every couple of months as they add new streaming platforms. It's a 100% free. There's nothing to purchase. It's simply ad supported entertainment. At a time when people are worried about inflation, I see this as potentially an inflation resistant stock because it's a 100% free service. If parents find that they're running out of money and they have to cut back on Netflix or Amazon Prime, this would be a really solid option for them because it doesn't cost them anything and it will help them entertain their children. On top of that Genius Brands has over 65 merchandising licensees in the global market with over 500 product SKUs. I actually bought some of the toys myself just to do some due diligence on them and they're 100% legit. They have over 20 licensees for animated content in over 90 countries. Over 450 product SKUs anticipated to launch over the next 12 months with top-tier manufacturers such as Mattel, Bentex Group and McMillan for publishing. They have all the right connections and, in my opinion, all of the right ingredients to be a really serious competitor in the children's entertainment space if not potentially a market leader eventually. The CEO and Chairman Andy Heyward, he's been involved in a lot of shows that we are all familiar with from our past. Andy Heyward is a multi-Emmy-winning producer of children's entertainment. He is the former Chairman and CEO of DIC Entertainment where he produced more than 5,000 episodes of children's entertainment, including the Real Ghostbusters, Inspector Gadget, Alvin and the Chipmunks, G.I. Joe, Hello Kitty's Furry Tale Theater, Sonic the Hedgehog, the Super Mario Brothers Show, Sabrina the Animated Series, Strawberry Shortcake, Care Bears, Captain Planet, Teddy Ruxpin, The New Archies, and dozens of more. He has such a strong track record with incredible shows like Inspector Gadget and a lot of experience and connections and people and talent within this company, involved in the production of the shows and the business overall. Also, Genius Brands has mentioned that when they are producing their cartoon shows, they always aim for toyetic, merchandisable characters, that way they can sell products and branded merchandise just to have multiple revenue streams. Then here are the three pillars that Genius Brands identifies as the most valuable parts of their business. First of all, the growing portfolio of brands, they have 11 properties in various stages of development, production, or distribution, and over 450 distinct program episodes delivered or in production, plus additional episodes in various stages of production and pre-production. In terms of consumer products and distribution, 65 consumer product licensees globally with over 500 licensed product SKUs for them to sell merchandise and swag related to their shows in over 90 different countries. In terms of their platform distribution, Kartoon Channel is currently in over 100 million US households on Comcast, Cox, Dish, Sling, and numerous platforms including Amazon Fire, Apple TV, Roku and more. Massive distribution and tons of households have the ability to just download this app and plug into the shows. Basically, super valuable brands, good distribution platform that they own as well as products being licensed out to toy manufacturers to make additional revenue from these well-known and well-liked characters. In terms of products, they sell Llama Llama and Rainbow Rangers but what I see as the number one growth driver for this company right now is Stan Lee's Superhero Kindergarten. This show has been an absolute blowout success for them. Episodes one, two, three and four have all gotten over 2 million views each and some of them even crossed 3 million views. Here's what they said about that.

"Network hours watched went up 941% week-over-week to almost 350,000. Unique users went up

1841%, new application installs went up 465.9%."

This show is a huge marketing tool for them and it's already allowing them to drive new app installs and get new users for their app by establishing partnership with Arnold Schwarzenegger and leveraging the connections that he has. He's already been on Jimmy Kimmel as well as the Kelly Clarkson show talking about this show and there's over 20 episodes that are going to be coming out every single Friday. Think this is going to be our growth driver for this company for the foreseeable future. Then when Shaq's Garage comes out, that's going to push this to even newer heights. When we take a look at the financials of this company, this is why I become even more excited about this stock. As of December 31st, 2020, they had $108 million of assets on the balance sheet and only $15 million of total debts. They have a ton of cash on the balance sheet - over a $100 million that they're just going to put towards production and acquiring of different media assets. But the interesting thing to me about that is if there's a $100 million of cash and only 300.32 million shares, that means for every share of Genius Brands purchased, there's 33.3 cents in the bank, which is an astronomical amount of cash especially considering that this stock trades for under $2 per share. There are always unforeseen risks involved here, and this is a company in 2020 had under $2.5 million of revenue. Almost no revenue to speak of, really just looking to acquire a strong user base and get people enjoying their content. That is a lot of the reason why the stock has just not moved is because they're not focused on revenue right now. Honestly, $2.4 million of revenue for a company valued about a third of a billion dollars, a lot of people are saying that is ridiculous and it's just way too high. However, my argument is that the value is within the amount of cash the company has, as well as Andy Heyward and his connections as well as the value of that Stan Lee brand, that easily gets you to a valuation of a third of a billion dollars, but that is strictly my opinion. Genius stock had a lot of short interest that has been going up over the last couple of weeks. I'm not saying there's potential here for a short squeeze but what I'm telling you is that there's a lot of big money shorting this stock. So, I think a lot of what's been going on has a lot to do with short selling and not as much to do with underlying fundamentals. But this is why it's important to do your own research and due diligence on your own before making an actual investment yourself. The short interest on the stock is certainly interesting to me because if there is a massive rally with this stock there is the potential there for a squeeze to occur which we saw that happened earlier this year back in February, we had a pretty good squeeze there on this stock buck. I actually don't want that to happen because this is a stock, I want to own for the next 5 to 10 years.

At number three is the most speculative one and the smallest company it's called Grom Social, trading under the symbol, GRMM. This one trades on the over-the-counter markets, and it is a media tech and entertainment company. They also have launched a social media platform for kids under 13 years. They're also involved with the production of animated films and TV, and they have a web filter service for schools and government agencies. A couple of different interesting business segments to unpack here. First of all, to understand the business model of Grom Social, let's take a look at their different subsidiaries. Grom Social is basically the social media aspect of their website on iOS and Android, which allows kids to interact with their peers safely and in a good closed off environment that's ideally safer than these mainstream social media platforms for adults. They also have the Grom educational services, which is the web filtering for schools and governments and private businesses. They also have Top Draw Animation which is an award-winning producer of top-quality animation and a leading source of 2D animated programming. Then the newest acquisition there is Curiosity Ink Media, which is a cross platform and media and entertainment company serving kids and families with ground-breaking original storytelling content. What they're planning on doing is they're launching an app called MamaBear which is going to tie in directly with the other Grom Social apps, which is going to allow parents to be in complete control of their children. For example, if your child had a Grom Social profile, you from your own phone would be able to track all of his activity and see exactly what he's doing to make sure he's being safe online. That is what's really cool about this. I completely agree that social media is dangerous for children, and I love this company that's putting together an interesting solution for that problem. On top of that, here's a couple of other cool features involved with their social media app. You can send doodles to your friends, which a lot of those looks like some of the features that Apple has on their products. So, they're seem to copycat a lot of this, but since they're launching an app just for kids, it might just work for them because it's a new space. Also, when people will try to make their kids to use a children's version of Facebook, I think people would be much more likely to trust a newer company like this, rather than getting involved with Facebook who has lost the trust of so many people, so many times repeatedly over the years. Then, there's the TikTok style chapter posts which they basically have created a children's version of TikTok since that video app is very popular among kids. It's just meant to be a safer environment where parents will ultimately be able to keep track of their children's activities. Grom Social is the only COPPA compliant social media app for children under 13 that allows them to record and share chapters. As of right now, they're the only kids safe TikTok style app that allows you to share videos, which I think is an interesting moat that they may have here but not much of one because anybody could do this. There's not much of a moat or something protecting them from competitors, but if they're able to garner enough attention and kids ultimately start using it, well, they're going to share it with everyone and with their friends and it should grow like that. But it's hard to tell whether or not Grom Social is going to come out ahead with a kid's social media app or is Facebook or Instagram just going to try to get into that market themselves. I think people would be more willing to trust a new company rather than Facebook, but we'll have to see how that plays out. Then as part of that top drawer animation studio they've produced content for Disney, Kartoon Channel Scholastic, Nickelodeon, Warner Brothers Pictures, Hasbro, and Dreamworks. There's a number of the different shows that they were involved with. Then with their newest acquisition, Curiosity InK Media, they're getting something called Santa.com which we'll talk about shortly as well as a couple of other franchises as well as curiosity books imprint - just a lot of different brands here with interesting potential. There's a lot of overlap here between

Genius Brands and Grom Social because they're both involved very heavily in children's entertainment. Grom Social Enterprises which recently entered into a binding letter of intent to acquire Curiosity Ink Media, announced that Curiosity will debut Santa.com, an online hub where kids and adults can experience classic holiday joy in a one-stop modern digital holiday venue in quarter four of 2021. The online holiday hub represents an opportunity to tap into the growing holiday retail market projected to top 1 trillion this year. It's certainly interesting to see what this could become. I did some research, and it looks like christmas.com sold for about $3 million. So, I think this is a multimillion-dollar domain name that they now have in their possession. For kids, Santa.com will offer a special place to register with their wish lists, take a tour of the north pole and schedule a virtual visit with Santa. Santa.com aims to de-stress the holidays for parents by offering them tools to discover purchase and send personalized gifts that are arrived, wrapped, tagged, and ready to give all from the comfort of their home. This just seems super interesting. Grom Social they're all over the place and really, they just need one of these things to work well for them in order for this company to do well, especially when they're only being valued at under $40 million. However, there is a very high degree of speculation involved with a stock trading at this size. There's limited information available and it's hard oftentimes to get the real idea of what is going on with a company this small. They've also been involved with some influencer deals and they are sponsoring Caroline Marks who is a professional surfer in the upcoming 2022 special Olympics. That is a good sign in my opinion too. If we look at the financials, they have about 17.8 million of assets and 8.5 million of debts. The balance sheet is not nearly as appealing as Genius Brands, but not too much debt to speak up and about a two to one ratio of assets to debt which I like to see.

LIABILITIES AND STOCKHOLDERS' EQUITY				
Current liabilities:				
Accounts payable		$	1,350,911	$ 808,520
Accrued liabilities			1,736,185	1,651,482
Advanced payments and deferred revenues			742,258	627,082
Convertible debentures, net – current			1,908,168	4,828,656
Derivative liabilities			68,753	77,584
Related party payables			213,233	462,137
Lease liabilities – current			294,058	263,252
Total current liabilities			6,313,566	8,718,713
Convertible debentures, net of loan discounts			1,274,743	505,000
Lease liabilities			404,853	633,098
Loans payable			253,912	–
Other noncurrent liabilities			189,758	227,229
Total liabilities			8,436,832	10,084,040

Income Statement ...

⌂ Get access to 40+ years of historical data with Yahoo Finance Plus Essential. Learn more

		September 30, 2020	December 31, 2019

The Very Good Food Company trades on the

Toronto Stock Exchange under the symbol of VERY.B or from the United States you can buy them on the over-the-counter markets under the symbol VRYYF. If you're in Canada, Quest Trade is a pretty solid brokerage that you could use. If you're in the United States Charles Schwab is the brokerage that I used to purchase my shares. With Genius Brands the good news is it's a NASDAQ listed stock so you can buy it pretty much anywhere. I bought my shares on Robinhood, but you could also buy it on Charles Schwab or pretty much any other commission-free trading app if you wanted to. Lastly, Grom Social is another over the counter stock trades under the symbol, GRMM. I purchased my shares on Charles Schwab.

Chapter 5
Tesla Stock
Analysis & Fair Value

Despite the recent focus on the controversy surrounding Elon Musk's pumping, he is still the CEO of the world's largest car company Tesla, a firm that is arguably just as controversial in the investing world. Depending on who you talk to, Tesla is either most overvalued company in the stock market that is due for a correction down to 100 dollars per share or is a multi-trillion-dollar company in the making that deserves a share price of 3,000 dollars. In this chapter I will be covering my analysis and fair price of Tesla for those who are still deciding on the company from a valuation standpoint. Let's see if the tech sell-off in early 2021 has created a buying opportunity for Tesla or if a price of about $580 as of May 21st is still pricing in too much of the company's future growth. When analyzing Tesla's business, there are three main business segments to look at; the most well-known and largest, accounting for close to 80 of 2021 Q1 revenues is their automotive segment. Tesla's lineup currently includes four in production battery electric vehicles the Model S, Model Y Model 3 and Model X. Falling in the premium vehicle category, Tesla cars come in a wide variety of base prices, depending on their driving range and features. All new vehicles include Tesla's autopilot features for self-driving, which currently stands at level 2 of driving automation - meaning the vehicle control both steering and acceleration, but the driver is still in charge of monitoring all tasks. According to Musk, the company is very close to achieving level 5 autonomous driving in terms of basic functionality the maximum level with no driver interaction. Even if the company is able to make this breakthrough in 2021, it will still be a while before we see the tech roller to test the cars as it will take some time to set this up in actual vehicles and for the public to come around to the idea. Tesla has made some headlines recently with crashes linked to the autopilot system, making some question their self-driving technology. The increase in crashes involving Teslas is simply the result of the huge jump in their cars on the roads over the past few years in my opinion, as according to crash data in Q1 Tesla cars accounted for one accident for every 4.19 million miles driven in which drivers had autopilot engaged. In comparison data from the national highway traffic safety administration in the US States an automobile crashes every 484,000 miles on average, or more than eight times more often. In terms of market share, the firm dominates the US with 80% of newly registered battery electric vehicles in 2020 coming from Tesla. As of Q1 2021 however, Tesla's share in Western Europe has been struggling to keep up with the fast growth in the market and has fallen to 15% from a peak of 31% of the end of 2019. Many European legacy automakers like Volkswagen have been pushing for EVs harder than their American counterparts, making this a more competitive space. New reports are also suggesting that their Giga Berlin factory that will provide a much-needed source of local production in Europe will be delayed another six months until early 2022 and we could see Tesla's European market share continue to dip in the meantime. A key area for Tesla will be China - their second biggest market that accounted for 29% of Q1 2021 sales, up from 21% in 2020. There have been complaints recently from Chinese consumers about quality issues that could create some problems with regulators. Going forward as competition heats up in the country, sales in China will be important to watch for Tesla investors. Overall, sales for Tesla EVs are growing at an incredible parabolic rate as adoption picks up and the firm expands its number of gigafactories. Compared to American and legacy automakers from other countries, the firm also has amazing automotive gross margins of 26% as of Q1, that make this a very exciting young car company.

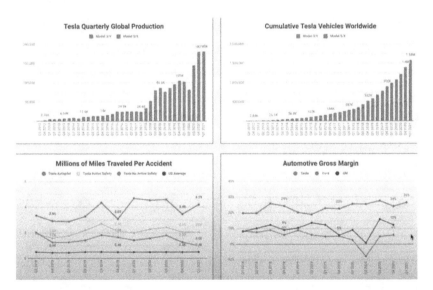

On a net basis, Tesla still doesn't make any profit from auto sales and to see how they've become profitable recently, we have to look at their second major revenue stream; regulatory credits. As a manufacturer of EVs, Tesla earns tradable credits for the development of their vehicles under government regulations that try to push automakers to sell zero emission vehicles. Automakers need to meet thresholds for the number of credits they earn in a jurisdiction with such regulations in place and if unable to, are forced to buy credits from another firm with an access like Tesla. Since they come at no cost to Tesla, the sale of these credits is 100% profits. In Q1 Tesla made $518 million from selling regulatory credits and only $438 million in net income, meaning they are only profitable right now because of these carbon credit sales. This has become the main point of many bearish theses on Tesla, since the credits are expected to become less lucrative in the near future, including that of Michael Burry. This famous investor who predicted the 2008 financial housing crisis has recently released a fairly large put position against Tesla, as he thinks the reliance on carbon credits impedes the company's long-term prospects. According to Tesla's CFO, this will not be a material part of their business in the long term, and I have to agree that with the trajectory the company is currently on in terms of sales growth and gross margins, profitability is easily obtainable without the credits in the not so distance future. In Q1 Tesla converted 1.2 billion of their cash reserves into Bitcoin and later sold 10% of it to supposedly prove the liquidity of the cryptocurrency and when researching on this, I wanted to see if they made a mention of the profits from this in their Q1 earnings presentation. If we go into the presentation and try and search for Bitcoin, there are only two results. Both of which are for statements describing the net cash outflow from the purchase. But if we look above on the financial summary page, I was surprised to find a statement that in fact the company had made $101 million on the sale of Bitcoin.

If we highlight the area though we see that this statement has been deliberately not been written in text and appears to be added as an image making it unsearchable. I'm not going to speculate as to why Tesla has decided to do this, but it certainly is deceptive in my mind and appears to be a way to attract less attention to another margin boosting source of income for the company. Despite this and Elon's recent antics, I do think the Bitcoin purchase was a good move by the company with inflation on the rise and looking at recent Tweets, it doesn't appear that the company has sold the remaining 90% of their Bitcoin so far. To complement their growing margins, Tesla has an amazing balance sheet relative to other US automakers.

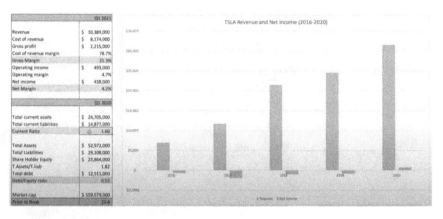

With a nice amount of cash on their balance sheet, Tesla has a current ratio of 1.66 - meaning short-term obligations are not a concern and they also have enough cash on hand to cover their total debt of $12 billion. A debt decade ratio of 0.52 also puts Tesla among the best in the industry and is one of the reasons many people are bullish on a younger firm like this, over a legacy automaker like Ford, who has three times more debt than shareholder equity. Tesla is priced very high because of this and their growth potential however, giving them a massive price to book ratio for a car company of 23, compared to only 1.5 for Ford. Overall, for Q1, Tesla's quarterly net margins were their highest to date at 4.2%, thanks to the regulatory credits mentioned earlier. The excellent financial health of the company is a huge turnaround from 2018 when at one point Tesla was bleeding so much money, that it was close to dying according to Musk. To come up with a fair price for Tesla, I have made a discounted free cash flow model that estimates the company's growth out to the end of 2030.

Discounted Free Cash Flow (DCF) Model

	2016	2017	2018	2019	2020	2021E	2022E	2023E	2024E	2025E	2026E	2027E	2028E	2029E	2030E	Terminal Value
Revenue	7,000	11,759	11,461	24,578	31,536	49,200	65,900	82,906	104,468	131,625	165,847	199,017	238,820	286,584	343,901	
Revenue Growth		68.0%	82.5%	14.5%	28.3%	56.2%	33.9%		26%					20%		
Net Income	-675	-1,962	-976	-870	690	3,006	5,057	8,291	10,446	14,479	18,243	23,882	28,658	37,236	44,707	
Net Margin	-9.6%	-16.7%	-4.5%	-3.5%	7.2%	6.1%	7.7%	10%	10%	11%	11%	12%	12%	13%	13%	
Operating Cash Flow	-133	-61	2,098	2,405	5,943											
Capital Expenditures	1,440	4,080	2,320	1,440	3,240											
Net Debt Issued	1,718	5,468	85	322	-2,488											
Free Cash Flow to Equity	155	-673	-133	1,287	215											
FCFE/Net Income	-23%	34%	14%	-148%	31%	50%	70%	80%	90%	90%	100%	100%	110%	110%	120%	
FCFE Estimate						1,503	3,540	6,633	9,402	13,031	18,243	23,882	31,524	40,960	53,649	785,285
Discount Rate	10%															
Perpetuity Growth	3%															
Discount Factor						1.0572	1.1629	1.2793	1.4071	1.5478	1.7026	1.8728	2.0601	2.2661	2.4928	2.4928
Present Value of Future FCF						1,421	3,044	5,185	6,682	8,419	10,715	12,752	15,302	18,084	21,522	316,677
Market Cap	419,604															
Shares Outstanding	963.11															
Fair Price																

First, I've used analyst expectations for revenue in full year 2021 and 2022, which currently stand at 49.3 and 65.8 billion as of mid-May. This would mean a significant boost to revenue growth which is only 15% and 28% in 2019 and 2020 but would be 56% and 34% in this year and the next. Analysts also anticipated jumping at margins, based on their current EPS projections that would give Tesla margins of 6.1% and 7.7%. Until 2030, I have made my model with 26% revenue growth in the four years from 2023 to 2026 and then a slowdown to 20% until 2030 as Tesla gets bigger. While some may think 20% growth is a bearish take, it's important to remember that high growth rates are much easier to keep up when you're a company making 31 billion per year compared to 165 billion. I also see net margins slowly growing over the decade and have them at 13% by 2030. Although this is higher than any other car company, with Subaru having the highest of 7.5% average over the past five years, I do think that Tesla has already displayed with their high gross margins that once economies of scale come more into play, they should be able to achieve higher net margins. I also think that with the expansion of their battery and other higher margin business initiatives, that Tesla will be more profitable than the typical car company. Looking at Tesla's past free cash flow equity isn't overly helpful, since they have not been netting him positive outside of 2020, but we do have FCFE tenant income last year of 31%. This should continue to increase over time in my opinion and then begin to plateau later in the decade, and I've assumed these ratios for the model. At a discount rate of 10% and perpetuity growth of 3%, we can discount these future cash flows back to their present value and some for a fair market cap of $420 billion. At 963 million shares outstanding, Tesla has a fair price of 435 dollars per share according to the model. I feel that this is fair for Tesla as it captures their excellent growth potential and also isn't assuming the best possible scenarios for the company where many things would have to go their way in order for it to be accurate. With this fair price, we do see that Tesla is currently trading at a premium about 25% at a price of $580 per share and offers average returns of 6.8% until 2030.

TESLA, INC. (XNAS:TSLA)			

Fair Price	$ 435.78
Today's Price	$ 580.88
Margin of Safety	25.0%
Annual Return to 2030	6.8%

	2030E
Revenue Est	343,901
Net Margin	13%
Net Income Est	44,707
Shares Outstanding Est	1,400
Share Price (From FP)	$ 1,086.30
Market Cap	1,520,824
P/S Ratio	4.4
P/E Ratio	34.0
Share Price (From TP)	$ 1,447.99
Market Cap	2,027,190
P/S Ratio	5.9
P/E Ratio	45.3

Assumptions	
Avg Revenue Growth '23-'30	23%
Avg Net Margins '23-'30	11.5%
Avg FCFE/NI '21-'30	92%
Discount Rate	10%
Perpetuity Growth	3%
2030 Shares Outstanding (M)	1,400

Tesla was turning at this level back in late 2020 so it's not impossible that we will see another buying opportunity for the company if inflation and interest rate news continues to hurt growth stocks. As a quick comparison of today's price and the fair price, let's take a look at what price multiples we could expect based on the revenue and net income assumptions for 2030. At the 10% required rate of return for the model, Tesla's stock price in 2030 is 1086 dollars and assuming dilution with 1.4 billion shares outstanding, their market cap will be 1.52 trillion. This gives Tesla a price to sales ratio of 4.4 and a price to earnings ratio of 34. This is still very high among automakers, which generally trade at a PS ratio around or below 1 but does give Tesla a PE ratio below what we currently see for the S&P 500. Based on this, it's clear that Tesla will need to maintain their high margins to commit a valuation higher than traditional automakers or diversify more into their battery and other endeavors. If we were to expect the same 10% rate of return when buying a today's price, Tesla would have a price of $1447 per share in 2030, or a market cap of about 2 trillion. In this case, the firm would have a price to sales ratio of 6 and a PE ratio of 45. This is a bit too rich in my opinion and means Tesla would really have to differentiate themselves from their auto business, but for someone who thinks that this is reasonable, then maybe Tesla is still a buy today for your risk tolerance. In my mind, there's still a little bit too much of their future growth priced in at the current valuation, but if we see more weakness in growth stocks over the summer, there could be some buying opportunities for Tesla to come. On the technical side, things are looking shaky at the moment, with Tesla having recently broken its 200-day moving average and was seemingly stuck below this without any bullish news.

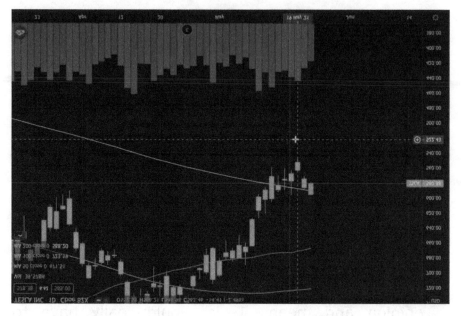

The chart for Tesla doesn't scream a buy to me alongside the fundamentals and I think right now is the time to sit out and wait to see how things develop, rather than rush into a trade on this stock. We could see a breakout on promising inflation numbers, so definitely something to keep an eye on.

Chapter 6
Top 5 Stocks for Double Digit Returns

With analyst estimates for rebounding economic growth in 2021, we can have new all-time high returns and really take your portfolio to a new level. In this chapter I will discuss five stocks to buy for higher upside. First, I want to show you the returns expected in stocks of each sector.

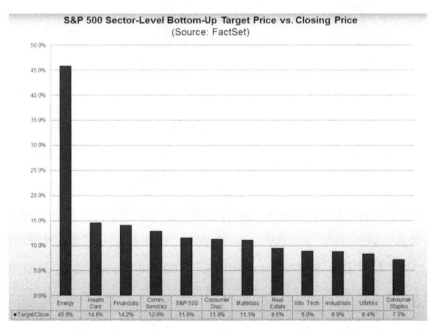

S&P 500 Sector-Level Bottom-Up Target Price vs. Closing Price
(Source: FactSet)

	Energy	Health Care	Financials	Comm. Services	S&P 500	Consumer Disc.	Materials	Real Estate	Info. Tech.	Industrials	Utilities	Consumer Staples
■ Target/Close	45.9%	14.6%	14.2%	13.0%	11.6%	11.4%	11.1%	9.5%	9.0%	8.9%	8.4%	7.3%

I like to look at this higher level first to see

which sectors of the economy that analysts think are going to do the best because it can really make investing in those individual stocks much easier. For example, analysts expect stocks in the energy sector to surge higher producing a sector level return of 45% over the next year. Knowing that, we can look for those best stocks to buy in energy to not only get that tailwind from the entire sector, but also an even higher upside shot on those best picks. The bounce in energy has been from the apocalypse and oil prices that we saw in 2020. The price of crude has rebounded to about $45 a barrel and with these production cuts that we've seen with a lot of the drillers if Opec plays nice and keeps its own supply off the market, we could see $50 of barrel oil again in 2021, which would be a huge sentiment boost for a lot of these companies. Analysts expect returns in energy to pretty much dwarf everything else, but I don't want you to go all in on this sector. There are a lot of other sectors here with some great potential and I think some individual stocks that can easily produce these returns of 20% or more. You've got expectations for stocks in the healthcare sector and financials to both produce a round of 14% returns on average. This is followed by an expected return of about 13% in communication services and 11% in consumer discretionary and material stocks. I like the health care and the financial space. Both have underperformed the market in 2020. Healthcare with an 8.6% return and stocks in the financial sector, so those banks, brokerage, and insurance companies they've posted the second worst return after those energy stocks. Healthcare it might seem counterintuitive though with all the focus on health nowadays, but the hospitals the doctors here have really been playing triage with their services. All those higher profit elective surgeries and the other services just been put on hold to care for these virus patients, so earnings have plunged. This could all change in 2021 and healthcare is one of my favorite long-term themes for investing. We're all getting older and spending more money on our health so this one has some great demographic forces behind it. For the financial sector, this is another one of my favorite themes for 2021 and we're already up 33% in shares of Citigroup in our 2021 portfolio. The optimism here is really a function of two catalysts. At first the banks have taken tens of billions of dollars off their earnings to hold his cash in what's called a loan loss provision account. This is a special cash reserve that the banks use to cover those estimated loan defaults if the economy gets bad, and it's meant that earnings have just cratered this year. If we get any kind of an economic recovery though in 2021, they reverse all that, they move that cash back into earnings and surprise on the upside along with big increases in their dividends. The second catalyst for financials here is in interest rates and really how they make money. For banks it's the difference in those rates paid on deposits, so those short-term rates and what they collect on those longer-term loans. The interest rate on the 30-year treasury bond plunged to a record low of 1.2% this year so even with those short-term rates near zero banks just aren't making any money. It's not just the banks either in the financial sector but insurance companies - they sit on those mountains of cash to pay those claims, but they're not getting any return on those safe investments like bonds and money market funds. Analysts expect the long-term rate to edge back up to around 1.7% in 2021 and if it can even get back to that % so where it was in 2019, that would be a boom to earnings for these banks. Hence those are the sectors I'm watching for 2021 returns. But you want those individual stocks to buy for those double-digit returns. Right now, stocks with the highest return potential are in that energy sector and some of these shares have actually already come up as well. For example, we've got a 44% return on our shares of Diamondback Energy, that's ticker FANG, and a 54% return on Devon Energy, that's ticker DVN. I do think there's still some good upside left in those shares of Diamondback Energy, but I don't want you to be a 100% in one sector. As well as energy stocks might do in 2021, I want to give you a list of five stocks across different sectors that are going to give you those double-digit returns but also some diversification. I researched both Morningstar and Credit Suisse for their top recommendations as well as some of my own favorites for a short list of the five best.

First on our list of 5 best stocks to buy tech leader Broadcom ticker AVGO and surprisingly not only does this one offers a great upside but also a 3.2% dividend yield. Through acquisitions, Broadcom has patched together one of the broadest leaderships in tech from smartphone components to wired infrastructure and to storage and semiconductors. If you want one tech stock that's going to benefit from some of the strongest trends like robotics, internet of things, and 5G, this is going to be it. But whenever I see a company built on that acquisition model, so buying up all these other companies, I run straight to the financial statements to make sure that it's not getting in over its head in debt. Broadcom has over 43 billion dollars in debt, which is about twice the equity, but also has over 8.3 billion dollars in balance sheet cash, so leverage is quite a bit lower than at first glance. The company generates over 6 billion in operating earnings a year, against just 1.7 billion in interest. Another metric that gives me that assurance on that leverage. What I really like about the company besides the catalyst that I'll highlight next is that not only is this company growing sales at a solid pace, but it's learning how to do that and how to be more efficient to boost earnings. Sales grew by 8.3% last year but the company was able to grow those operating earnings by 13.5%, which just is an amazing spread, given Broadcom size and those recent acquisitions.

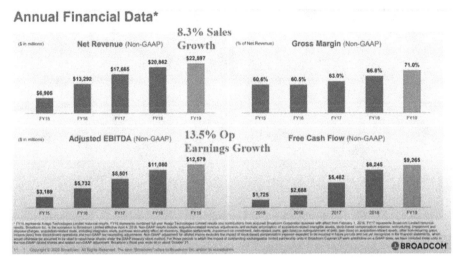

Annual Financial Data*

The release of the apple 5G should help boost sales and many of the company's products are primed to benefit in that work from home trend. The big catalyst here I think is going to be that transition to 5G. With the new 5G technology, you can get thousands of devices on any local network, versus the dozens of devices that you might be able to cram on there in a similar 4G network. That's going to drive the IoT revolution but it's also going to mean a lot of network congestion and a spike in demand for those kinds of RF filters that Broadcom excels in.

Earnings Summary

Next Earnings Date: 12/10/20

Earnings are probably the most closely followed aspect of a firm's income statement as an indicator of profitability. Also referred to as the net income for a specified period of time, earnings are equal to a company's after-tax income on the income statement. The net income is calculated by taking revenues and adjusting for depreciation, interest, taxes and expenses incurred through business operations.

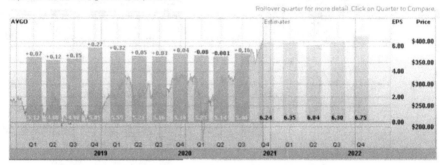

Earnings are expected 17% higher over the next year to $24.93 a share. Though I think it gets closer to $26 per share earnings the shares can trade between 18 to 20 times earnings with good investor sentiment, which puts us at a price target of around $500 a share.

Next on our list is called Anthem, ticker ANTM, isn't the largest healthcare insurance but it is one of the largest with over 42 million members in 23 States and it is the largest single provider of blue cross blue shield coverage. United Health is by far the larger insurer but here's why I like Anthem. Just a little bit more and why I actually put it into our 2021 portfolio. Anthem is in just 23 States versus United Health's national coverage but at 42 million members it's a close second to those 49 million members covered by UNH. It's because in the States where it operates, Anthem has a much deeper market share, upwards of a third of the market in each of those States. It's got an exclusive license with blue cross and 14 of those States which is arguably the most trusted franchise in health insurance. This just all works to give Anthem a lot more negotiating power with its providers, helping to lower costs pass some of those savings onto its customers and keep some of it for higher margins. With the election behind us and most likely split control of congress in 2021, that uncertainty around health care stocks has really cleared up. We could see marginal changes to the regulation, but I think the worst is off the table and healthcare is one of my favorite sectors in both the near term and longer term. Revenue grew at a 7% pace over the last three years which the company was able to then turn into a 20% annual earnings growth.

Long-Term Focus on Value Creation

Key Financial Metrics: *5-Year Performance*

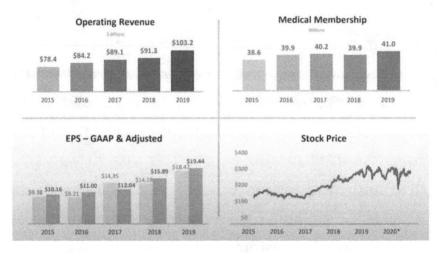

For the coming year earnings are expected lower by just about 1% to $22.48 per share. But management has a strong history of beating these expectations. On a price to earnings of 18 times a multiple the shares traded at just last year I think this one gets back to 404 dollars a share really quickly.

Fedex, ticker FDX is a best of breed in the industrial sector. FedEx is the world's largest global express shipping company and the demand picture here is just amazing. Most companies have to figure out a way to create that demand for their product before they can expand their operations, but for

FedEx that demand is just booming already. E-commerce sales spiked 37% in the third quarter and hit 16% of total retail sales last year from just under 12% previously. That trend to shopping online has been boosting sales for FedEx for years but gave it supercharged growth in 2020 and the momentum is just going to keep on going.

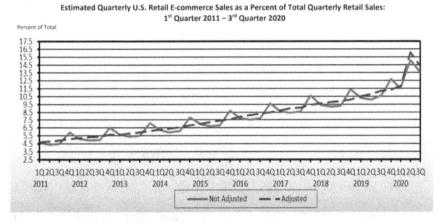

Estimated Quarterly U.S. Retail E-commerce Sales as a Percent of Total Quarterly Retail Sales: 1st Quarter 2011 – 3rd Quarter 2020

While discussing ecommerce shipping trend, I might say the shares are a little expensive here, but we've got another catalyst that isn't fully baked into these shares yet. With the Covid vaccines coming out, we are about to move into the biggest distribution problem in modern history. Not only do we need to get those vaccines to 7.8 billion people around the world and FedEx is already ramping up for that, but the two earliest vaccines from Pfizer and Moderna need to be kept at very cold and very specific temperatures. The problem is this; for example, Pfizer is distributing its vaccine in special deep freeze boxes of a thousand doses each. Those doses have to be kept at a specific temperature and used within a certain time frame after opening the box, but you've got a lot of rural towns that just won't be able to distribute all thousands of those doses. They just don't have the demand for it, so to avoid the waste in a vaccine that's going to be in very short supply anyway, I think you get a lot of local governments using that express delivery to move these boxes around the state wherever they need them. The company beat its Q3 earnings estimates by 81% and earnings are expected to jump 37% over the next four quarters to $15,51 per share. Between that long-term trend to e-commerce and this year-long boost from the vaccine, I think the share price can easily keep going to a price target of 350 dollars a share.

Macerich, ticker MAC, I hear a lot of people talking about Simon Property Group also and I truly believe if you're looking for a rebound play in this mall operator space, I would rather you be a Macerich then in SPG. Macerich owns 29 class a regional mall along with another 19 malls as part of partnerships and then 12 non-mall properties. That's a total of over 50 million leasable square feet and averages $800 in sales per square foot, which is well above the average for mall property space and really just speaks to the quality of assets. The company sold over four billion dollars in lower quality malls over the last eight years, so it really went into this whole pandemic for that quality. Sales per square foot were down only 10% in the third quarter and occupancy held up at 91%, which is really amazing considering that retail apocalypse. On that comparison with its larger competitor in the mall space, a Simon Property Group I like Macerich better because it doesn't seem to be getting mixed up in that retail business like Simon Property is which is bidding on a lot of the bankrupt stores like JC Penney's - it's kidding into the retail business. Instead Macerich just focusing on staying a landlord to these malls and finding new tenants like Amazon and distribution centers. Even on a lower dividend payment which was cut earlier in 2020 to protect the cash flow these shares are still trading at a 5.5% dividend yield. Macerich is just paying out just 25% of its funds from operations to cover that dividend so once some of this uncertainty comes out of the economy, I think that dividend jumps back up. With any of these rebound stocks, especially those mall operators you want to look at the balance sheet to make sure that the company has enough cash to pull through this thing. Macerich increased its cash holdings to 530 million dollars, which is enough to cover 19 months of its total operating expenses so plenty of cash there and more than enough liquidity if it needs to borrow against some of those high-quality properties. Funds from operations this year are expected 34% lower to $354 million, so even after that big jump in the shares recently the stock is still only trading for 4.6 times FFO. I'm not saying this one gets anywhere near that $27 a share anytime soon, but this is a nice double digit return over the next year, plus a per share dividend that actually could double from here.

Diamondback Energy ticker FANG is one of the sole energy stocks where I think you could still get a 20% or maybe even a 30% upside even after the recent run. Shares of Diamondback Energy have doubled since the 2020 March low but the average analyst target of 55 dollars could still mean a 35% upside beyond the 3.7% dividend yield. Diamondback Energy has been aggressively cutting its rig count to bring those costs down and protect its cash flow. Capital spending is down 35% from its original 2020 plan and operating costs are looking really good.

Management reported cash operating costs of just $8.16 per barrel in in the second quarter, which is among the lowest in the industry. Those costs came down 20% in the second quarter alone and should help to beat this quarter as well.

Earnings Summary

Next Earnings Date: 2/16/21

Earnings are probably the most closely followed aspect of a firm's income statement as an indicator of profitability. Also referred to as the net income for a specified period of time, earnings are equal to a company's after-tax income on the income statement. The net income is calculated by taking revenues and adjusting for depreciation, interest, taxes and expenses incurred through business operations.

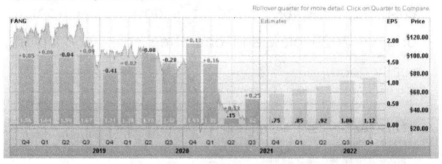

Annual Earnings and Estimates

	2019	2020	2021	2022	2023
		3.00	3.92	5.38	6.75

Rollover quarter for more detail. Click on Quarter to Compare.

The lower costs here have helped management commit to its dollar fifty per share dividend and the company is one of the best positions for that eventual rebound in oil prices. Earnings cratered to $4.15 per share over the last four quarters but management was able to beat those expectations by an astounding 69% last quarter. Analysts are expecting earnings to continue lower to about $358 per share over the next year, but even on this lowered guidance the shares are still just 11.5 times on that price to earnings basis. If we look at the trading history on this one diamondback traded for 14 times earnings last year and I think it can go back to that multiple for a 50-dollar price target. Beyond that, earnings are expected to rebound to $5.38 per share in 2022 for a potential 75-dollar price target. This is years of upside potential on this one and those dividends.

Conclusion

Thank you for purchasing this book. I hope this title has provided some insights of the Stock market and investing fundamentals.